THIS IS RHYTHM

by Ella Jenkins

with illustrations by Garrian Manning

Publications Director: **Eric Nemeyer**
Art Director: **Kristen P. Morgan**
Executive Director: **Mark D. Moss**
Cover & interior illustrations: **Garrian Manning**
Music typesetting: **Grey Larsen**

ISBN: 1-881322-02-5

Library of Congress Cataloging-in-Publication Data

Jenkins, Ella.
     This is rhythm / by Ella Jenkins; illustrated by Garrian Manning.
     p. cm.
     ISBN 1-881322-02-5 : $14.95
     1. Games with music. 2. Musical meter and rhythm--Instruction and study--Juvenile. 3. Music--Instruction and study--Juvenile.
     4. Rhythm--Juvenile literature. [1. Rhythm. 2. Musical meter and rhythm. 3. Songs.] I. Manning, Garian. II. Title.
MT948.J45 1993
781.2'24--dc20

93-24010
CIP
AC MN

Orders and inquiries should be directed to the publisher:
Sing Out Corporation, P.O. Box 5253, Bethlehem, PA 18015-0253   (215) 865-5366

THIS IS RHYTHM

This piece of work is
lovingly dedicated to my dear friend,
Gerry Glover, who introduced me
to Langston Hughes'
The First Book of Rhythms,
which inspired my creating
This Is Rhythm.

- Ella Jenkins

CONTENTS

Concerning THIS IS RHYTHM

This Is Rhythm was created with the intention of providing a musically therapeutic book and recording, aimed at elementary school grades. The book and recording are constructed to be used as teaching aids by teachers, parents, recreation workers, and musical therapists.

The book includes a group of rhythmic songs and chants with words, music and chord symbols. Sections in the book are devoted to the broader meaning and examples of rhythm, and an introduction to ten rhythm instruments. There is also an introduction to bell tones — using bells from many different areas of the world. The recording leaves room for children to identify the various bell tones. It is conceived as a way to stimulate them to think and recall places where they may have heard bells — bell tones related to their environment.

During the summer of 1960, I was made more aware of the great importance of different sounds and tones when I worked for eight weeks at a workshop with a group of blind children. By necessity, they depend almost entirely upon listening keenly. I spent two days exclusively working on bells with these children. The bells, some made of wood and some made of metal, were passed around from one child to another and I answered questions regarding their usage in various parts of the world. The children were completely absorbed for a long while as they held the bells close to their ears.

Two weeks after our first session with the bells, I brought them back to find out how much had been retained by the children. I felt a wonderful feeling of satisfaction as they easily identified the bells by listening attentively to the individual bell tones. I thought: "Another doorway of sound has been opened."

I love children and enjoy working with them. I want to feel that in some small or big way — using rhythm as my premise — that I may be instrumental in helping them grow into useful and uninhibited adults. I feel that there is a definite need for children and adults to relate to one another on a musical plane. Rhythm has been my means of achieving that kind of relationship. I found out quite early in my work with children and adults that they both respond most eagerly to rhythm — perhaps because it is such a basic ingredient. Exploring sounds is important to all of us at some stage in life, especially when we are children. We seem to need to express ourselves percussively.

I have discovered that when a child improves his "sense of rhythm" and explores a variety of sounds, he or she increases and expands his or her knowledge of many of the world's fascinations.

This Is Rhythm is for children or whoever makes use of it. To reap enjoyment in a relaxed manner, attain knowledge informally, and achieve creative expression is great abundance.

My heartfelt gratitude goes out to the following people for aiding in making This Is Rhythm a living reality:

- Members of the Children's Choir of the First Unitarian Church of Chicago, Reverend Christopher Moore, Director.
- Mrs. Betty Nudelman for her musical contributions to the original edition of this book.
- Mrs. Shirley Genther for her two lovely compositions, "Dark Winter Day" and "In Trinidad."
- Odetta Gordon's arrangement of "Little Red Caboose."
- Rhythm Band Instruments.
- Garrian Manning for all the illustrations in this new edition of This Is Rhythm

---

About your Rhythm Sticks:

The rhythm sticks included with this book can help you to encourage your child's participation and develop an interest in rhythm and music. When you use the sticks as a pair, consider clicking them together or rubbing the smooth one over the flauted (ridged) surface of the other to create a guiro effect (see page 50). The sticks can be used when you are reading the rhymes or singing the songs from the book to give rhythmic support. For extra sticks, send $3 per pair (postpaid) to The Sing Out Corporation, P.O. Box 5253, Bethlehem, PA 18015-0253.

A companion for this book and many other fine recordings by Ella Jenkins are available from Smithsonian/Folkways.
Write for a complete catalog and ordering information at:
Smithsonian/Folkways Recordings
414 Hungerford Dr., Suite 444, Rockville, MD 20850

RHYTHM

Is found in moving things - like waves in motion in the ocean.

RHYTHM

Is found in things that only seem to move - like pretty patterns on a zebra.
The black and white stripes seem to go from one row to another.

RHYTHM

Is found in many, many things...

THIS IS RHYTHM

A Heart Beating

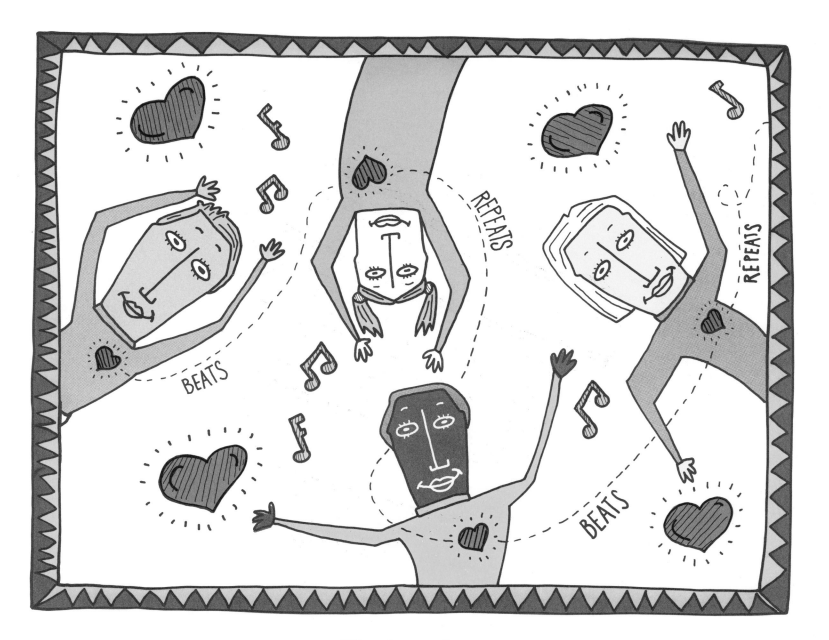

The heart beats
Then repeats
The heart beats
Then repeats

A Top Spinning

Better watch out
For your big toe
You can never tell where
The top might go

RHYTHM IS

Going

Foot steps here
Foot steps there
Foot steps almost
Everywhere

RHYTHM IS

A boat rowing

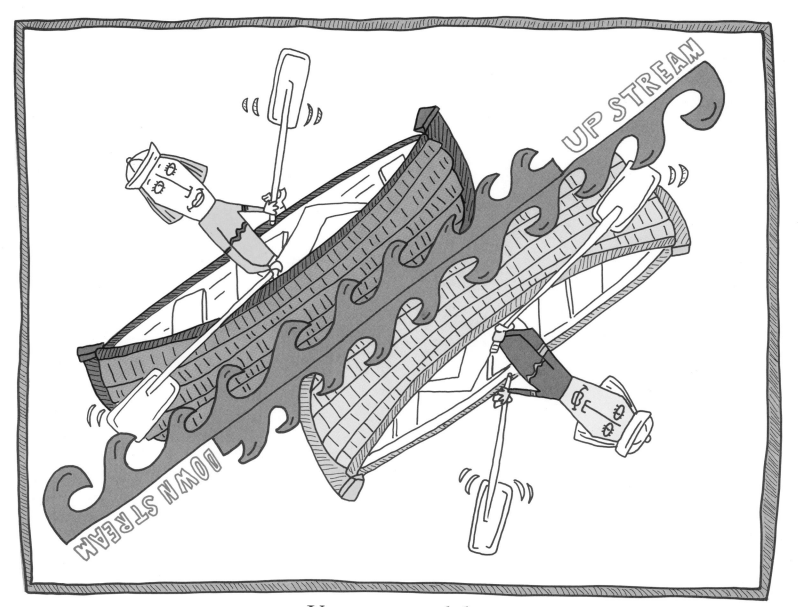

Up stream and down
All the way round
Up stream and down
All the way round

A flower growing

Yellow, pink, red or blue
Each flower says, "I love you."
Yellow, pink, red or blue
Each flower says, "I love you."

The wind blowing

Kites can climb higher
Than the tallest trees
When helped along
By a gentle breeze

A farmer hoeing

Across the fields
And back again
Hoping for a little rain

A woman sewing

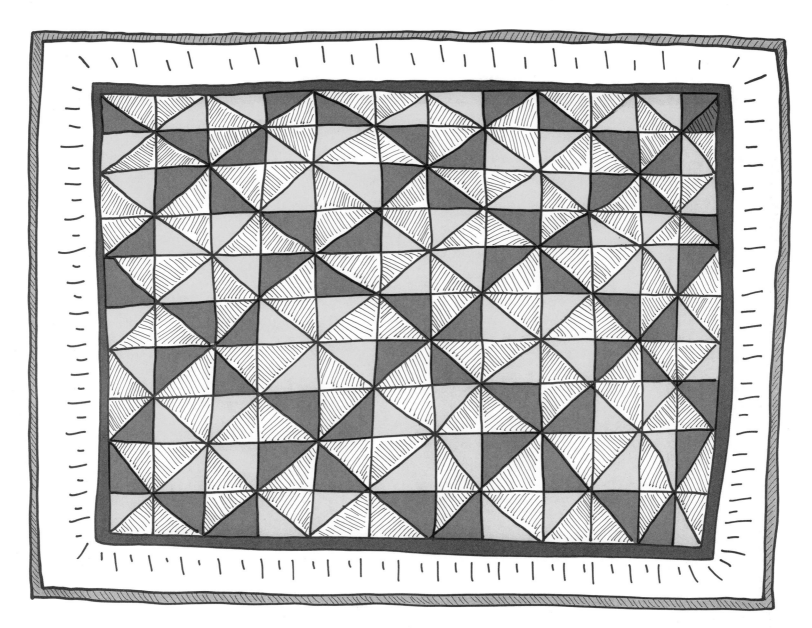

Here and there
A patch or two
Makes the blanket
Seem like new

Reading braille

Braille is a way of **printing** for the **blind**. This method of printing started a long time ago - in the year of 1829. It was invented by a man named **Louis Braille**. **Braille** is made up of many **raised dots**. When you move your fingers slowly back and forth across the braile, the little **dots** seem to **rise up** from the paper.

Do you have a friend who reads **braille**?
Schools where **braille** is taught will gladly share pages of
braille with **you.**

Rhythm is reading braille.

A dog's tail wagging

When your little dog
    Buries his bone
    He's never ever
    Far from home

Coffee bubbling when boiling

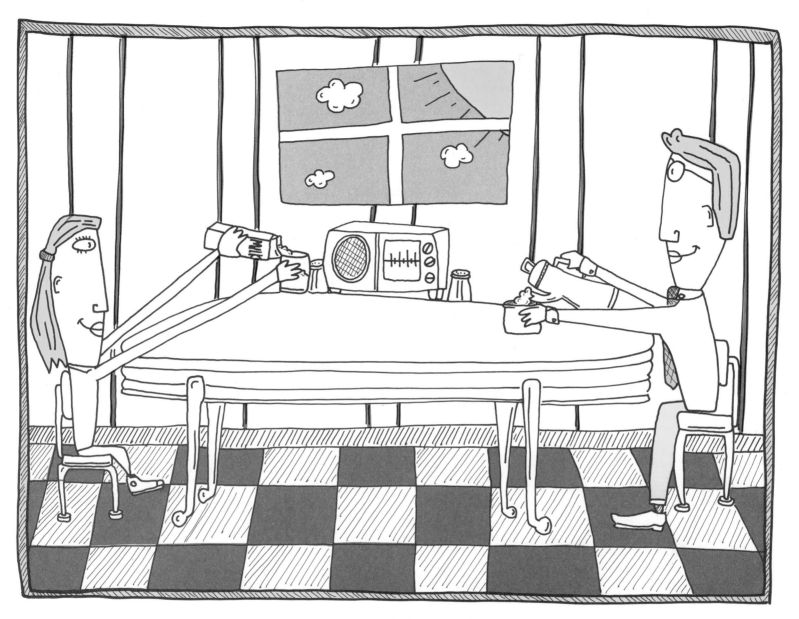

You may drink coffee
When you grow up
But now only milk
Should fill your cup

Paint dripping from a paint brush

Why don't **you** make up a poem about paint?

It's very easy - try it!

A clock ticking

Mr. Sandman, go away
I have other plans today
There will be no noon-time
Nap for me
I'm wide awake
As you can see ..... Ho hum zzzzzzz

THIS IS RHYTHM

1. Clapping your hands (clap, clap)
2. Snapping your fingers (snap, snap)
3. Jumping rope
4. Chewing food
5. Talking
6. Breathing
7. Blinking your eyes
8. Twinkling of a star
9. A ball bouncing up and down
10. The earth turning round and round

Why don't you add to this list?
How many examples of rhythm can you name?

Now that we have seen how **rhythm** runs in **many directions**, let's find out some **interesting** things about **rhythm instruments.** A **few** of these instruments may be **familiar** to you, however **some** of them will be **entirely new** to you.

Let's meet the instruments - one by one...

CONGA DRUM

I am the Conga Drum
Tap my head - I'm lots of fun
I am the Conga Drum
Tap my head - I'm lots of fun

The **Conga Drum** originated in **Africa** but may be found in countries like **Puerto Rico**, **Haiti**, **Cuba**, **Jamaica** and **Trinidad**, which are in the **West Indies** or in **Mexico** which is just south of the **United States**. Or you may find the **conga drum** right here in the **U.S.A.** because it is often shipped to many different countries around the **world**.

The **conga dance** also comes from **Africa** but it is well known and danced in many other countries.

You can tap out the **conga rhythm** on your **drum**. Start with your **left hand** and accent the **last beat**:

Left **right** left **right** left **right**
Dad's old fashioned root **beer**

CONGA DRUM

BONGOS

We are the little Bongos
One head high - the other one low
We are the little Bongos
One head high - the other one low

The **bongo drums** - or you may want to call them **bongos** - are small twin drums with one drum just a bit larger than the other.

The **small drum** is **high-pitched** while the **large one** is **low-pitched**. To play the **bongos** you must place them and hold them tightly between your **knees** and then tap them with your **fingers**.

The **bongos**, like the **conga drum**, are made and chiefly found in the **West Indies**. Many **bongos** are found in the **United States** because they have become such popular instruments here. People of all ages can tap out **simple rhythms** and have **fun**.

BONGOS

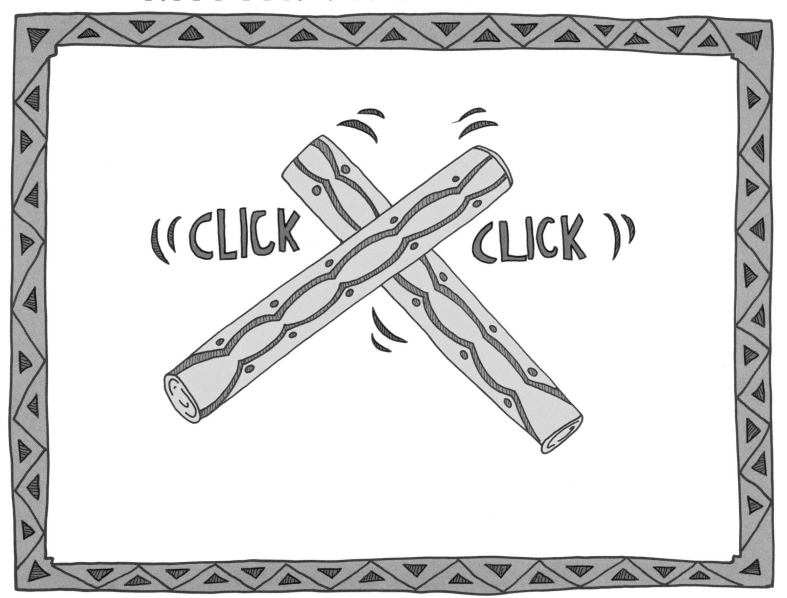

RHYTHM STICKS

We are the Rhythm Sticks
We go click click click click click
We are the Rhythm Sticks
We go click click click click click

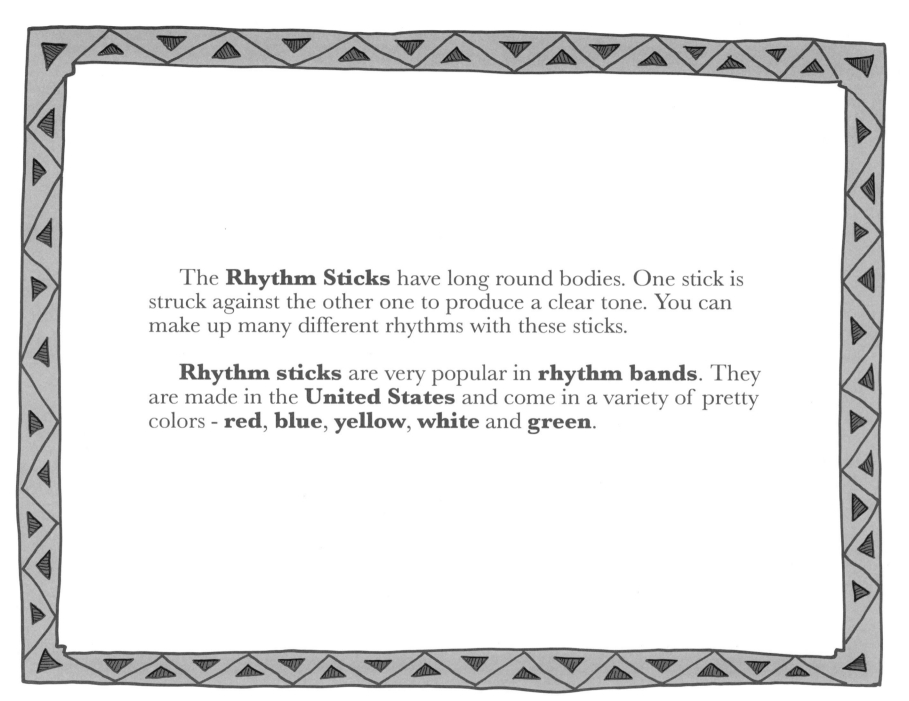

The **Rhythm Sticks** have long round bodies. One stick is struck against the other one to produce a clear tone. You can make up many different rhythms with these sticks.

Rhythm sticks are very popular in **rhythm bands**. They are made in the **United States** and come in a variety of pretty colors - **red**, **blue**, **yellow**, **white** and **green**.

RHYTHM STICKS

MARACAS

We are the maracas
Shake us chickee chickee cha
We are the maracas
Shake us chickee chickee cha

The **Maracas** are a pair of gourds that are filled with dry seeds. A **gourd** is a **vegetable growth**.

In order to make the **maraca**, the gourd must be dried in the sun. When the gourd is **dry** a hole is cut through the shell at both ends. Then it is scraped out, leaving only the **seeds** inside. After this is done the **handle** is put into the hole. The gourd is usually shaped like an **egg** but sometimes its shape is **round**.

Some **maracas** are painted with **glossy paint** some have **colorful pictures** drawn upon them and some of them have **beautiful carvings**.

To play the **maracas**, shake them back and forth, keeping the **seeds together** by having them strike the **front** and **back** walls of the shell.

The **maraca** is also a **West Indian** instrument.

MARACAS

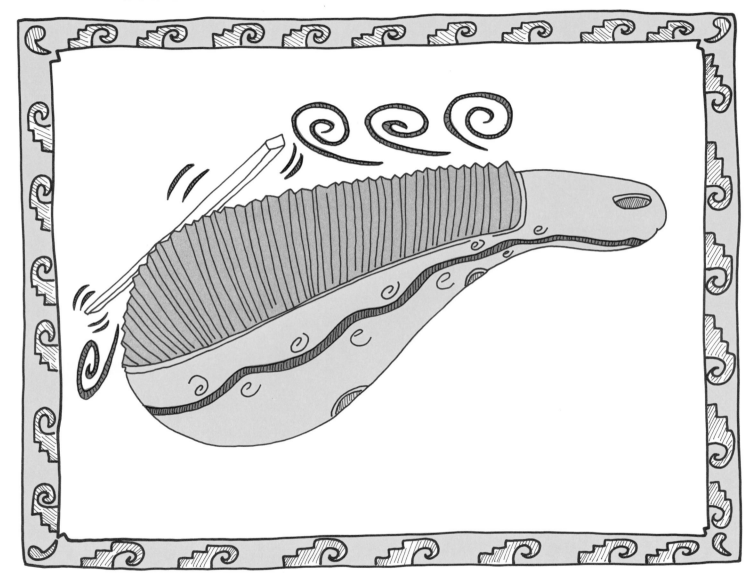

GUIRO

(pronounced "gwee-roh")

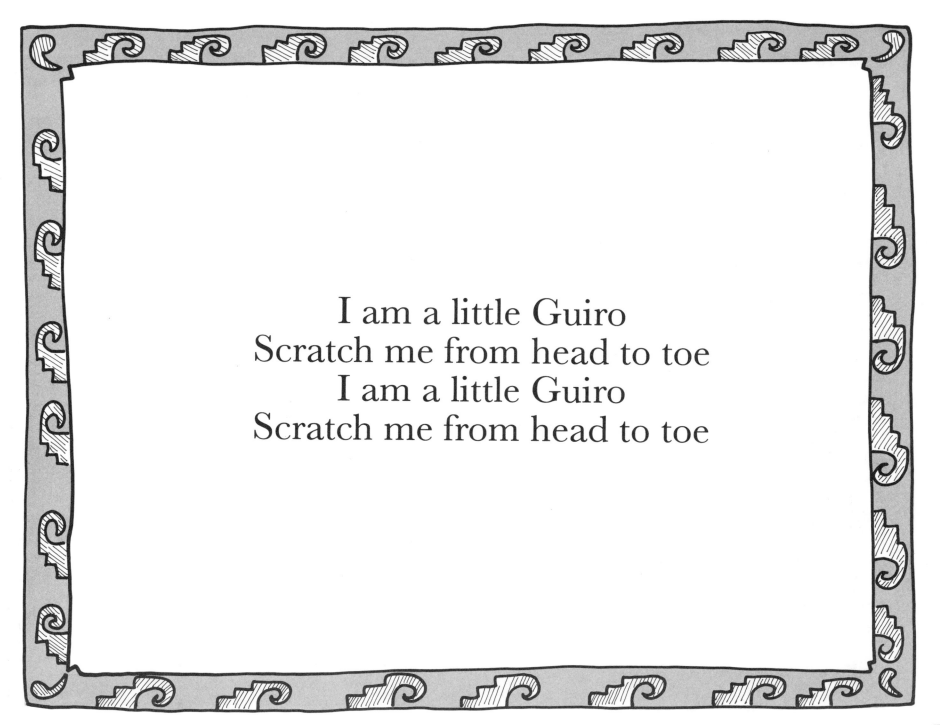

I am a little Guiro
Scratch me from head to toe
I am a little Guiro
Scratch me from head to toe

The **Guiro** is very much like the **maraca**, for it is also a **gourd**, and is scraped and dried out. The **seeds**, however, are **not** left behind as in the **maraca**, therefore the shell is entirely **hollow**.

The front side of the **guiro** is **ridged** and or **jagged** like a picket fence. It is scraped with a piece of **stiff wire** or a piece of **wood** shaped like a small **pencil**, to give a **scratching** sound. The back side has one or two holes for **holding** the **guiro**.

You can make **guiros** out of **wood** and **cow horns** instead of using the **vegetable growth**.

The **guiro** is another **rhythm instrument** from the **West Indies**. **Guiro** means **gourd** in **Spanish**.

GUIRO

53

COW BELL

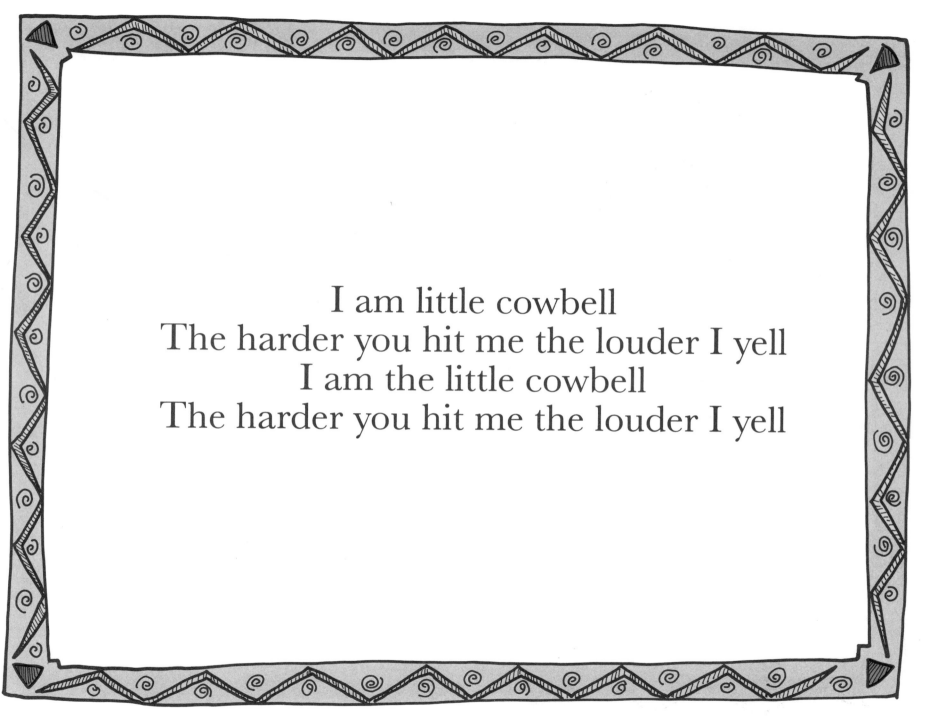

I am little cowbell
The harder you hit me the louder I yell
I am the little cowbell
The harder you hit me the louder I yell

The **Cowbell** is made of **copper**. It is usually played by holding the bell in the **palm** of one hand and being struck with a small **stick** or a **drum stick** with the other hand. Holding the **cowbell** in the palm of the hand prevents it from having a **ringing tone**. In order to make the ringing tone, hold the bell by the **handle** and **strike it**.

The **cowbell** is used a lot in **American orchestras** as well as in **West Indian orchestras**.

COWBELL

TONE BLOCK WOOD BLOCK

I am a little wood block
I sound like a tick tock clock
I sound like a tick tock clock
When played with the little tone block

The **Wood Block** is a hard block of wood about the length and thickness of a large shoe brush. There is a narrow **opening** on each side of the **wood block**. These openings make a **sound box**. The sound box is called a **resonator**. The **wood block** has a deep tone and it is to be struck hard in the center with a stick.

The **tone block** has a very **high pitch**. It is also struck with a stick, one with **a wooden ball** at the tip of it.

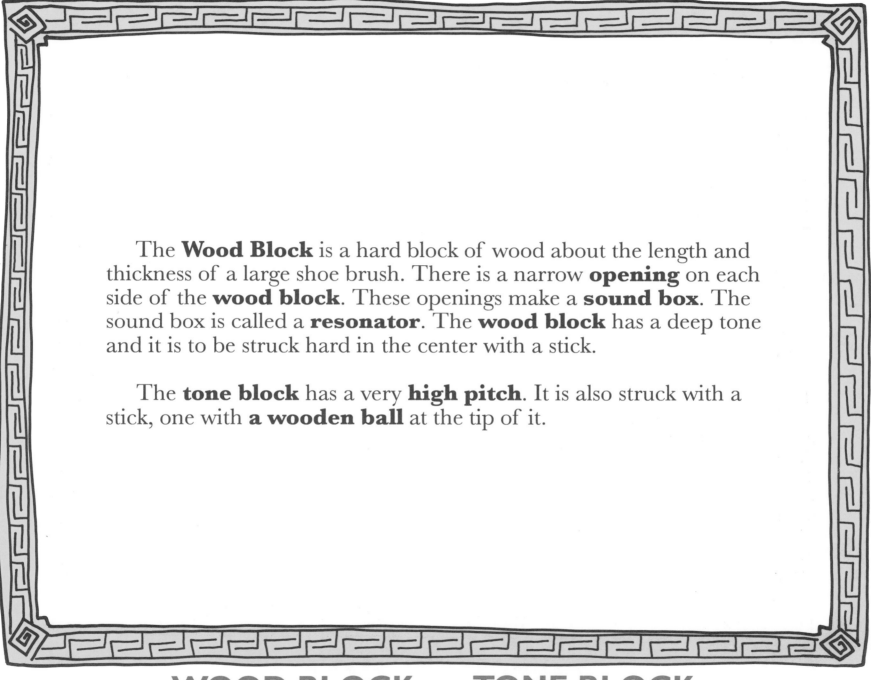

WOOD BLOCK   TONE BLOCK

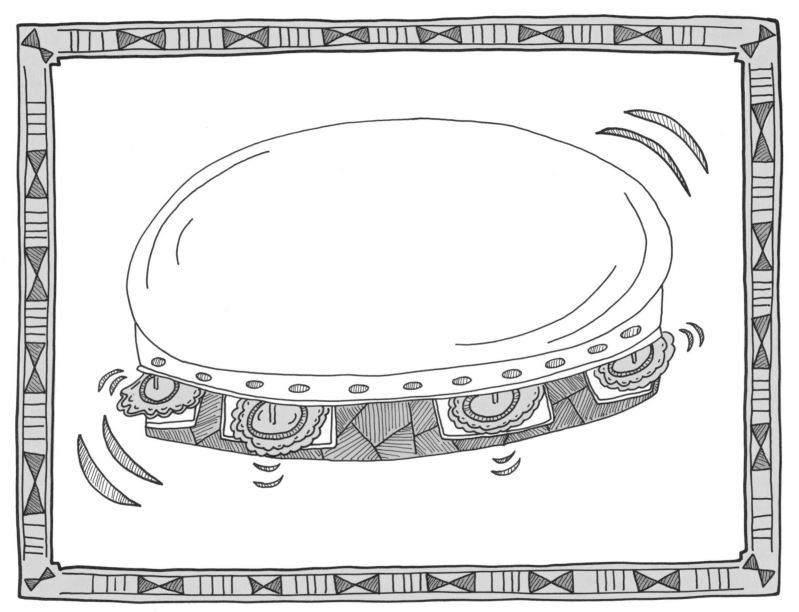

TAMBOURINE

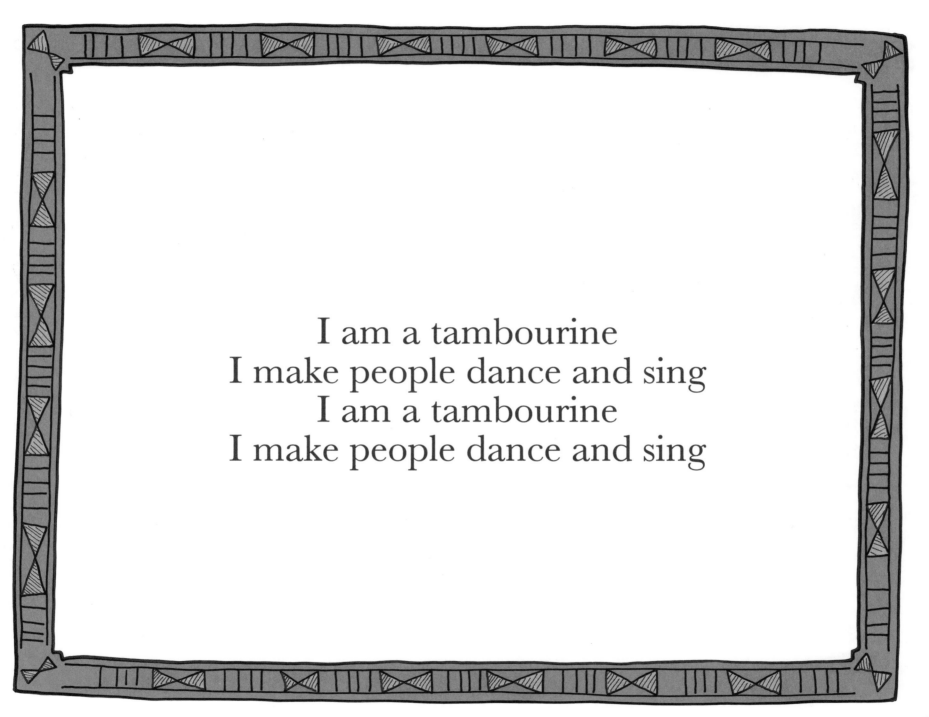

I am a tambourine
I make people dance and sing
I am a tambourine
I make people dance and sing

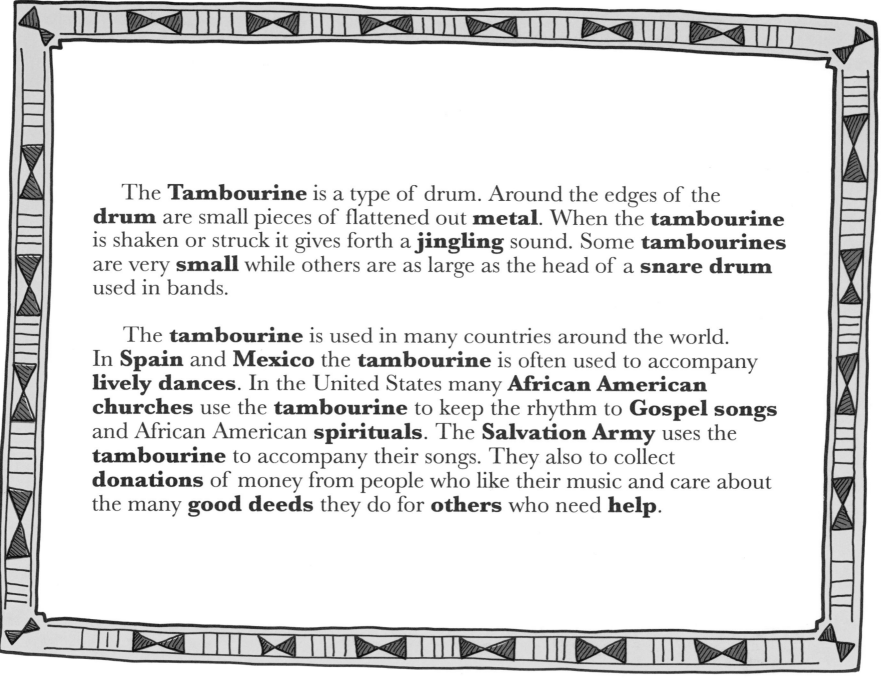

The **Tambourine** is a type of drum. Around the edges of the **drum** are small pieces of flattened out **metal**. When the **tambourine** is shaken or struck it gives forth a **jingling** sound. Some **tambourines** are very **small** while others are as large as the head of a **snare drum** used in bands.

The **tambourine** is used in many countries around the world. In **Spain** and **Mexico** the **tambourine** is often used to accompany **lively dances**. In the United States many **African American churches** use the **tambourine** to keep the rhythm to **Gospel songs** and African American **spirituals**. The **Salvation Army** uses the **tambourine** to accompany their songs. They also to collect **donations** of money from people who like their music and care about the many **good deeds** they do for **others** who need **help**.

TAMBOURINE

PLATE GONG

I am a little plate gong
My tune is ding ding dong
I am a little plate gong
My tune is ding ding dong

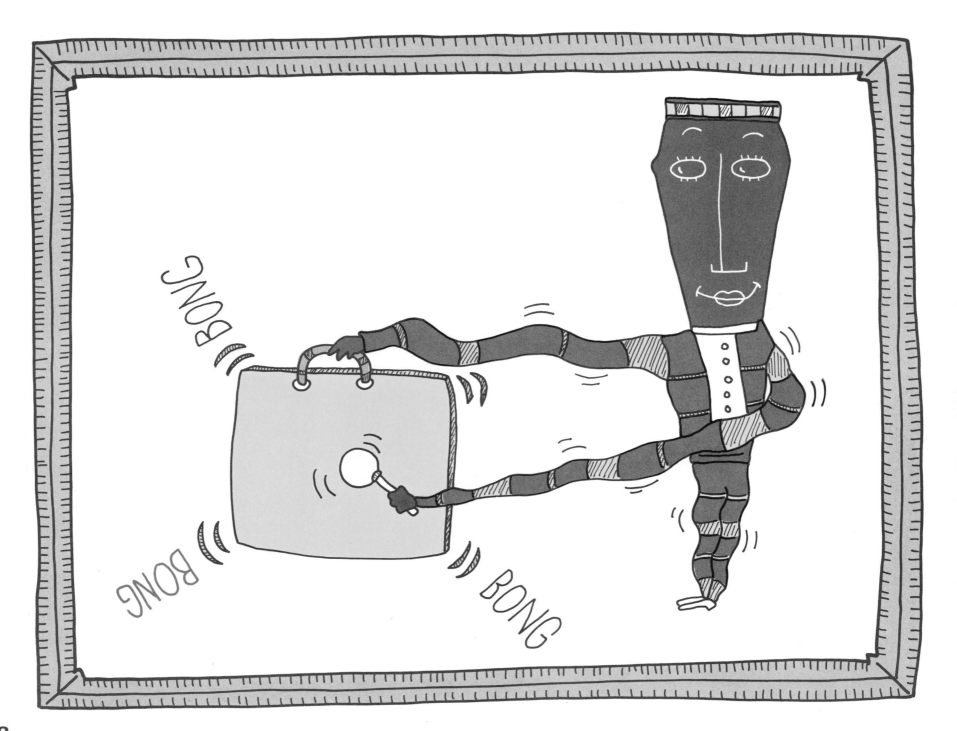

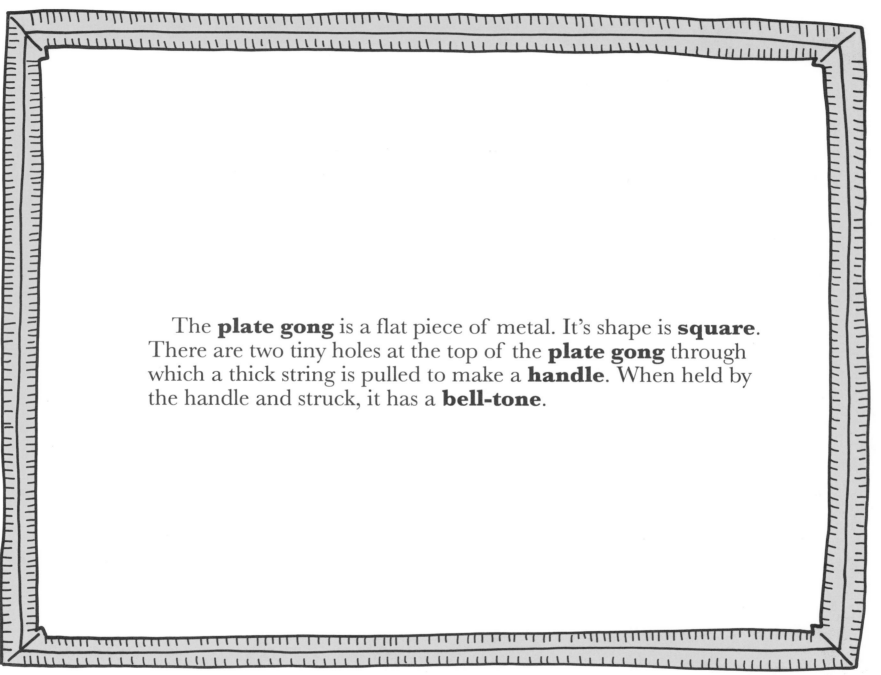

The **plate gong** is a flat piece of metal. It's shape is **square**. There are two tiny holes at the top of the **plate gong** through which a thick string is pulled to make a **handle**. When held by the handle and struck, it has a **bell-tone**.

PLATE GONG

When some people hear the **bell tone** of the **plate gong** they are reminded of a **ship's** bell or a **church** bell or a **fire** bell or an **alarm** bell or a **school** bell or a **door** bell or a **stove timer** bell or a **boxing match** bell or a **wrestling match** bell or a **chime clock** bell or a **clock on a court house** or a **curfew** bell (long ago) or a **dinner** bell or a **Sunday School** bell or a **bicycle** bell or a **"Good Humor"** bell or a bell **at the beach** or a bell **for the carry out boy in a restaurant** or a bell **in the dime store for signals** or a **railroad signal** bell or **Christmas** bells or a **walk "lite"** bell or bells **for when bridges go up** or a bell **cord at the gas station** or a **pony cart bell** or a **festival** bell or bells **on a sleigh** or a **merry-go-round** bell.

What kind of **bells** are you reminded of?

Here Are Some Bell Tones From Different Parts of The World:

First we'll listen to some bells from **India**. These bells are called **Bells of Sarna** and they come in many different shapes and sizes.

The next bells are **sleigh** bells. We might find them almost **anywhere** in the world, especially during the **winter holidays**.

Here is a bell made of **clay** from **Mexico**.

Now, a **copper** bell from **Africa**. Cattle wear such bells around their necks.

This bell should be familiar - it's the kind of bell we use at **dinner time**. Do **you** have a dinner bell in your home?

Let's now listen to bell tones from **Asia**.

This is a **wooden** bell from **Indonesia**. It is struck with a **wooden hammer.** This bell is also from **Indonesia** and is made of wood.

This bell tone comes from **China**.

Our last bell tone is from **Korea**.

LET·S BUILD A RHYTHM

First Group: tick tock, tick tock, tick tock, tick tock

Second Group: like a clock, like a clock, like a clock, like a clock

Third Group: go to sleep, go to sleep, go to sleep, go to sleep

Fourth Group: (spoken)
> Are you sleeping, are you sleeping
> Brother John, Brother John
> Morning bells are ringing, morning bells are ringing
> Ding, ding dong, ding, ding dong

First Group: Tick tock, tick tock (first group starts and continues)

Second Group: Like a clock, Like a clock (start on the third **"tick"** and continue)

Third Group: Go to sleep, go to sleep (start on third **"like"** and continue)

Fourth Group: Sings "Are you sleeping, etc. (Start on third **"go"** and continue)

Add the **Tone Block** for the **Tick**
Add the **Wood Block** for the **Tock**
Add the **Plate Gong** for the **morning bells are ringing**

HEAR THAT TRAIN

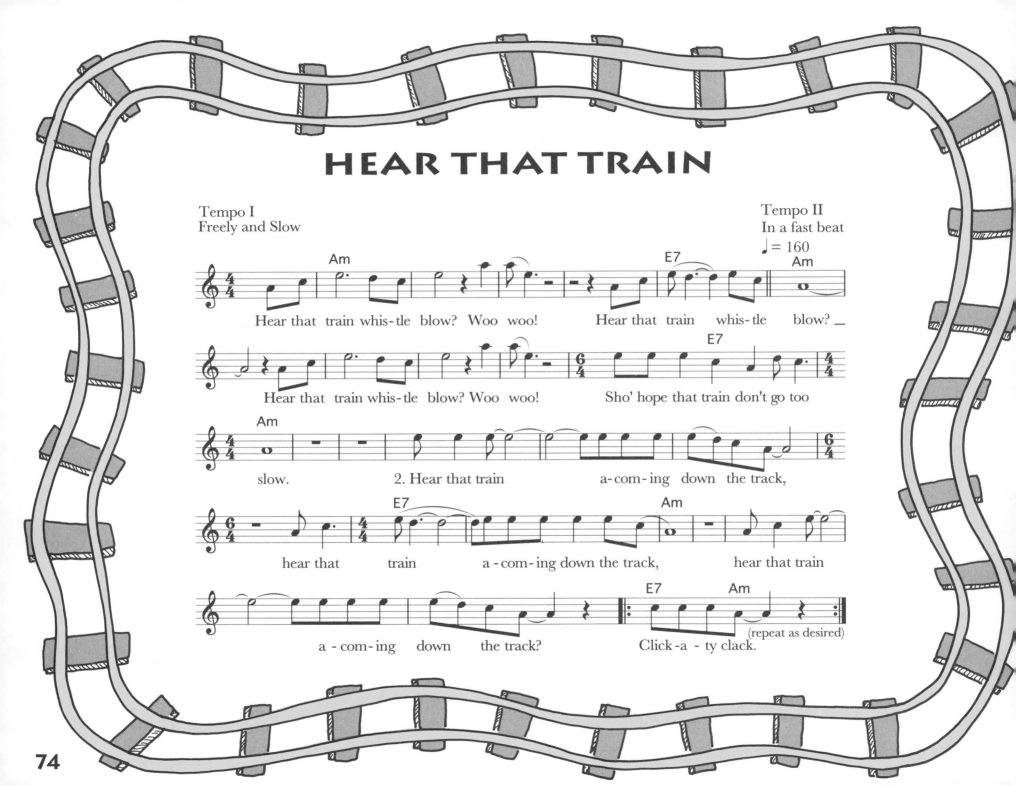

Hear that train whistle blow? Woo woo!
Hear that train whistle blow?
Hear that train whistle blow? Woo woo!
Sho' hope that train don't go too slow

Hear that train a-coming down the track?
Hear that train a-coming down the track?
Hear that train a-coming down the track?
Clickaty clack, clickaty clack, clickaty clack.....

CHICKA HANK

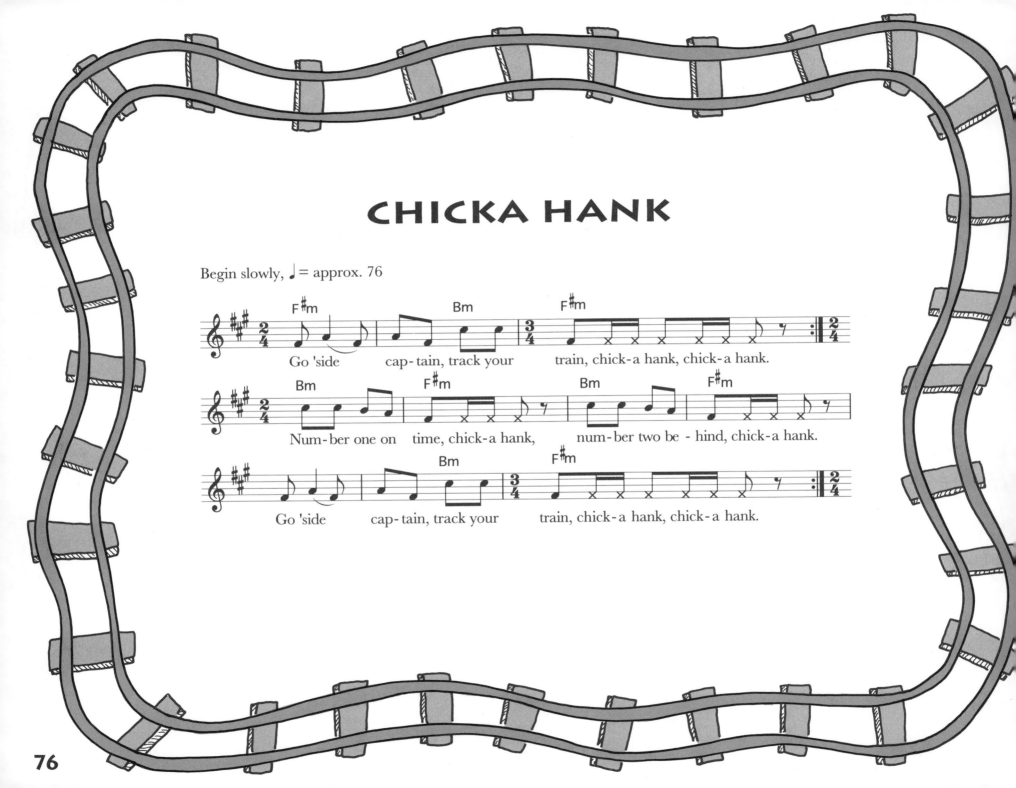

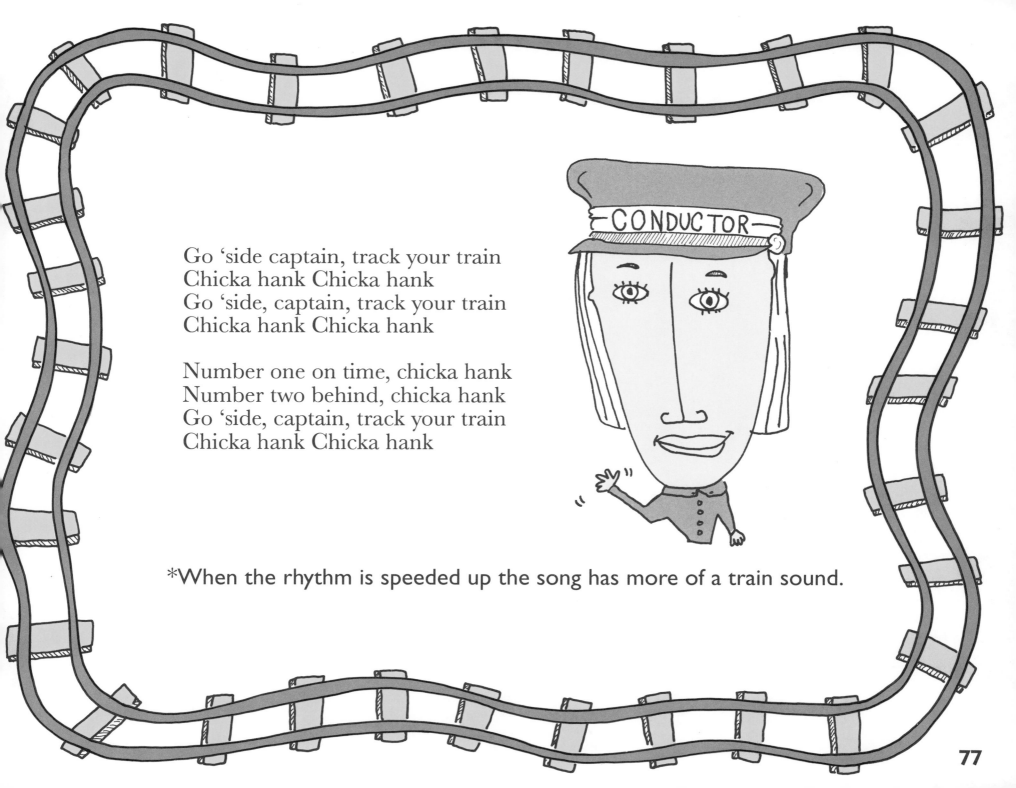

Go 'side captain, track your train
Chicka hank Chicka hank
Go 'side, captain, track your train
Chicka hank Chicka hank

Number one on time, chicka hank
Number two behind, chicka hank
Go 'side, captain, track your train
Chicka hank Chicka hank

*When the rhythm is speeded up the song has more of a train sound.

THIS TRAIN

Moderate, ♩ = approx. 126

1. This train is bound for glo-ry, this train is bound for glo-ry,

this train is bound for glo-ry. Child-ren, get on board.

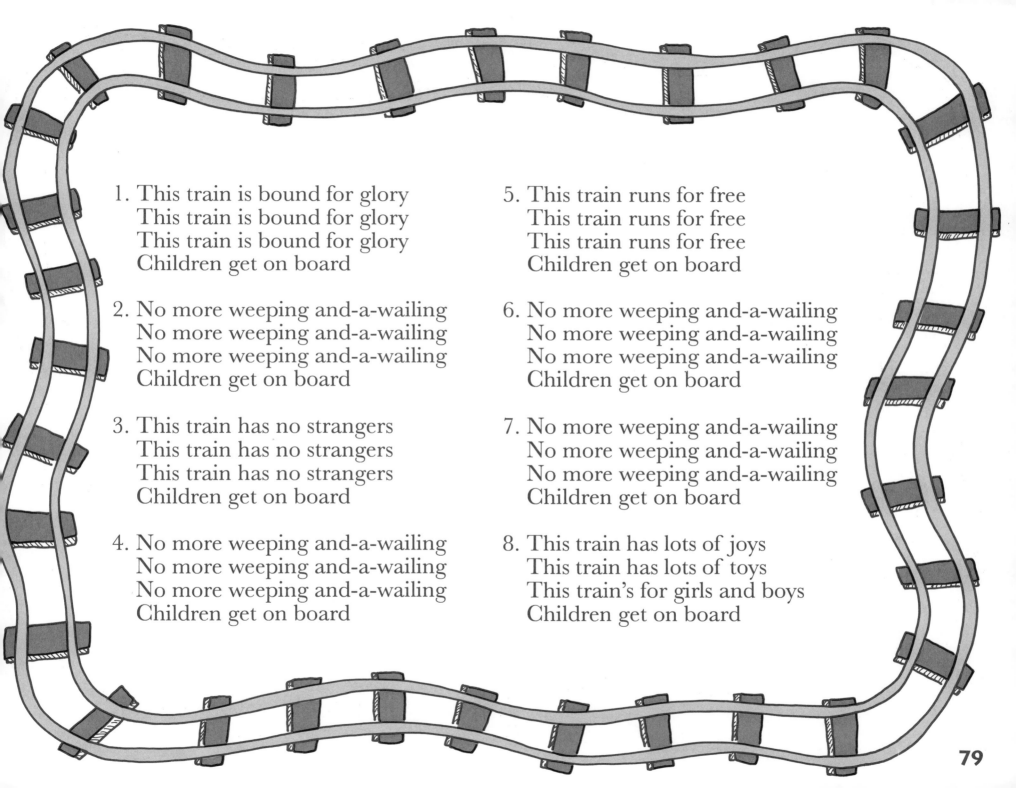

1. This train is bound for glory
   This train is bound for glory
   This train is bound for glory
   Children get on board

2. No more weeping and-a-wailing
   No more weeping and-a-wailing
   No more weeping and-a-wailing
   Children get on board

3. This train has no strangers
   This train has no strangers
   This train has no strangers
   Children get on board

4. No more weeping and-a-wailing
   No more weeping and-a-wailing
   No more weeping and-a-wailing
   Children get on board

5. This train runs for free
   This train runs for free
   This train runs for free
   Children get on board

6. No more weeping and-a-wailing
   No more weeping and-a-wailing
   No more weeping and-a-wailing
   Children get on board

7. No more weeping and-a-wailing
   No more weeping and-a-wailing
   No more weeping and-a-wailing
   Children get on board

8. This train has lots of joys
   This train has lots of toys
   This train's for girls and boys
   Children get on board

79

LITTLE RED CABOOSE

Moderate, ♩ = approx. 96

Lit -tle red ca - boose, chick-a chick-a, lit -tle red ca - boose, chick-a chick-a,

lit -tle red ca - boose be -hind the train, train, smoke stack on its

back, chick-a chick-a, go -ing down the track, chick-a chick-a, lit -tle red ca -

boose be -hind the train, train. Chick-a chick-a chick-a chick-a

chick-a chick-a chick-a chick-a chick-a chick-a chick-a chick-a choo.

Little red caboose, chick-a chick-a,
Little red caboose, chick-a chick-a,
Little red caboose behind the train, train
Smoke stack on its back, chick-a chick-a,
Going down the track, chick-a chick-a,
Little red caboose behind the train, train

Little red caboose, chick-a chick-a,
Little red caboose, chick-a chick-a,
Little red caboose behind the train, train
Smoke stack on its back, chick-a chick-a,
Going down the track, chick-a chick-a,
Little red caboose behind the train, train
Chick-a Chick-a Chick-a Chick-a Chick-a Chick-a Chooo

O WHERE O WHERE HAS MY LITTLE DOG GONE?

The second and third vocal parts can be sung simultaneously with the main song.

spoken: The merry-go-round
Has a musical sound
Up and down and
Round and round
Up and down and
Round and round.....

Oom pah pah, oom pah pah, oom pah pah, oom pah pah, etc.
Twiddle dee, twiddle dee, twiddle dee, twiddle dee

O where O where
Has my little dog gone?
O where O where
Can he be?

With his tail cut short
And his ears cut long
O where O where
Can he be?

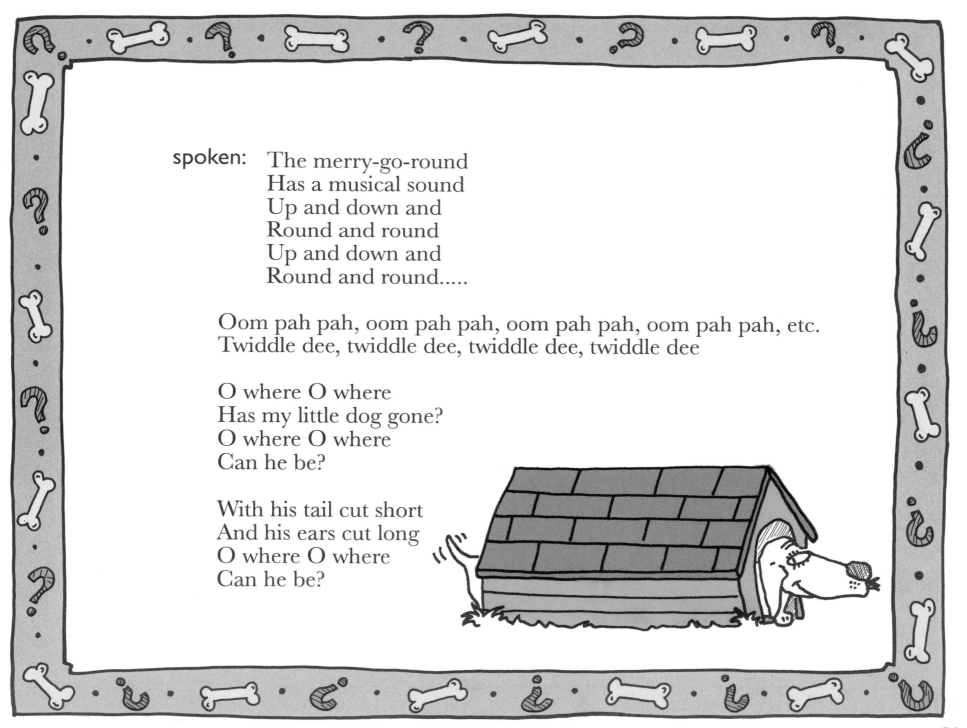

MY DOG HAS FLEAS

Oh goodness, oh gracious!
Oh goodness me
Oh goodness, oh gracious!
My dog has fleas! My dog has fleas!

I bathed him, I shaved him
O yes siree
I rubbed him, I scrubbed him
But my dog has fleas! My dog has fleas!

I tried all kinds of powders
Those fleas I tried to catch
But when my dog moves around
He begins to scratch....and then it's....

Oh goodness, Oh gracious!
Oh goodness me
Oh goodness, Oh gracious!
My dog has fleas, my dog has fleas, my dog has fleas

A RABBIT WITH A FLEA

Begin at a moderate speed, ♩. = approx. 144

There was a lit - tle rab - bit with a flea up - on its ear, there was a lit - tle rab - bit with a flea up - on its ear, there was a lit - tle rab - bit with a flea up - on its ear, and he flipped it and it flew a - way.

There was a little rabbit [1]

With a flea upon its ear [2] [3]

There was a little rabbit [1]

With a flea upon its ear [2] [3]

There was a little rabbit [1]

With a flea upon its ear [2] [3]

And he flipped it [4]

'Til it flew away [5]

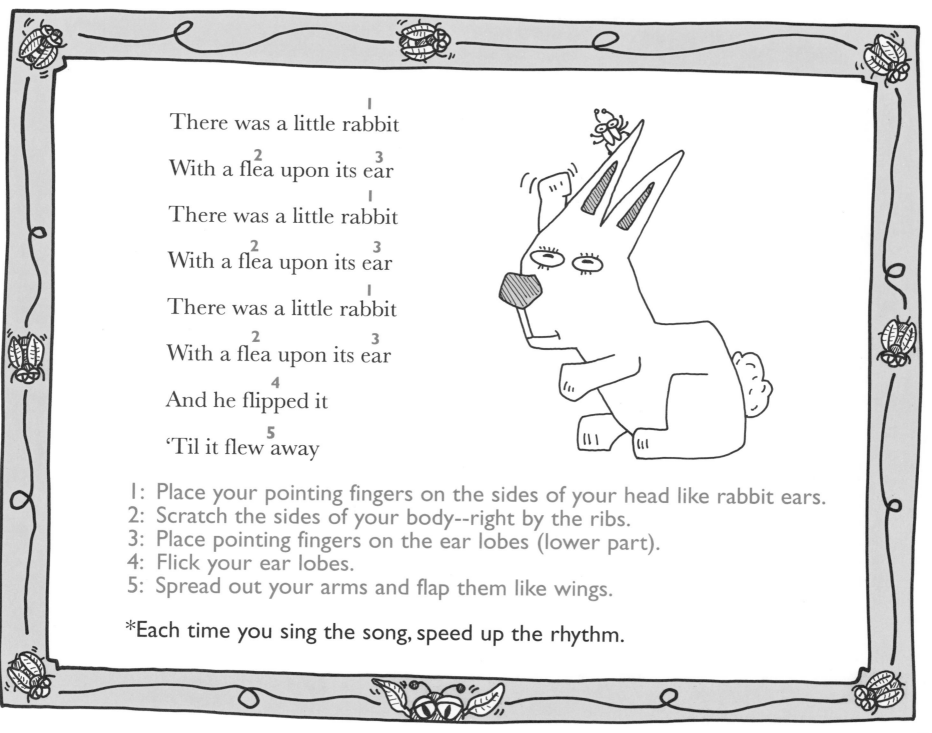

1: Place your pointing fingers on the sides of your head like rabbit ears.
2: Scratch the sides of your body--right by the ribs.
3: Place pointing fingers on the ear lobes (lower part).
4: Flick your ear lobes.
5: Spread out your arms and flap them like wings.

*Each time you sing the song, speed up the rhythm.

DARK WINTER DAY

by Shirley Genther

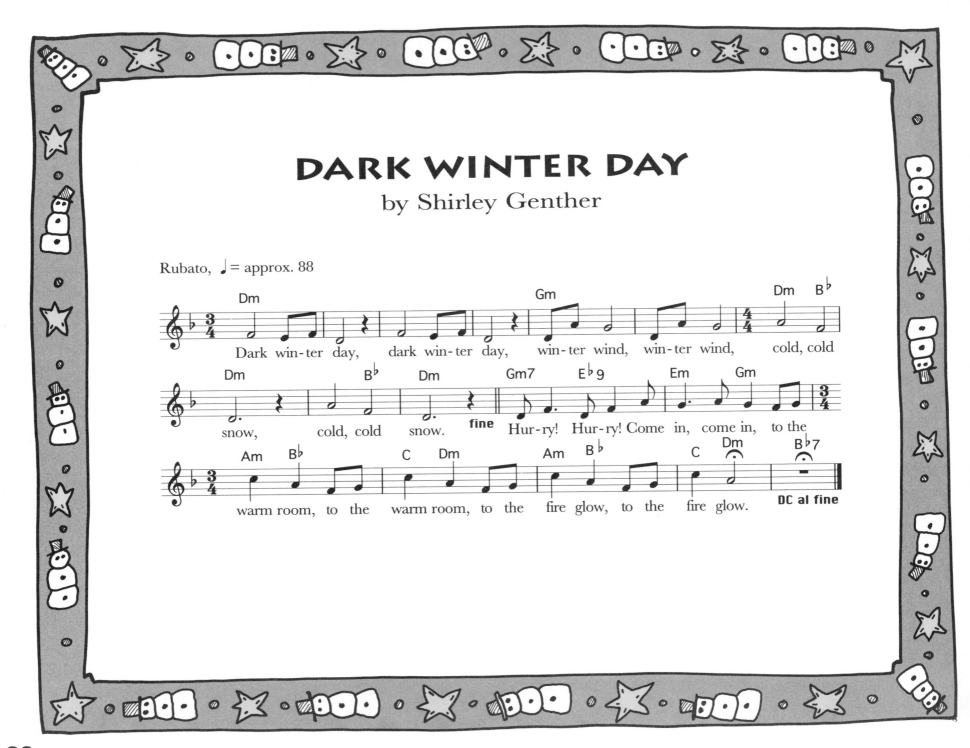

Dark winter day, dark winter day,
Winter wind, winter wind,
Cold, cold snow, cold, cold snow,
Hurry! Hurry! Come in, come in,
To the warm room, to the warm room,
To the fire glow, to the fire glow.
Dark winter day, dark winter day,
Winter wind, winter wind,
Cold, cold snow, cold, cold snow.

MEXICAN HAND CLAPPING SONG

Lively, ♩. = approx. 80

1. Ev-ery-one come right a-long, [clap, clap], let's learn a Mex-i-can song. [clap, clap]. Ev-ery-one come right a-long, [clap, clap], let's learn a Mex-i-can song. [clap, clap].

"SERAPE"

CLAP

1. Everyone come right along (clap clap)
   Let's learn a Mexican song (clap clap)

2. Muchacha means little girl (clap clap)
   Muchacho means little boy (clap clap)

3. Muchacha means little girl (si si)
   Muchacho means little boy (si si)

4. La la la la la la la (clap clap)
   La la la la la la la (clap clap)

5. Muchacha means little girl (O-lay!)
   Muchcho mean little boy (O-lay!)

6. Loo loo's sound good also
   Loo loo's sound good also

"SOMBRERO"

CLAP

*For variation, play melody on piano or another instrument without the use of the words, and use rhythm instruments sometimes instead of hand claps, etc. Also, speed up the rhythm now and then.

92

bad, he was bad, that bull, that bull, in Trin-i-dad, in Trin-i-dad. Tch tch tch tch tch tch tch tch

tch tch tch tch tch tch tch tch tch tch tch tch tch tch tch tch tch tch tch tch tch tch.

In Trinidad, in Trinidad,
A bull ran off, a bull ran off,
Just after ten, just after ten,
A mad, bad bull, a mad, bad bull,
He tossed a rabbit into the grass
And hit a wagon that was full of bananas, bananas, tomales, tomales, avocados,
   avocados, tomatoes, tomatoes, potatoes, potatoes, lettuce, lettuce, carrots,
   carrots, radishes, radishes, celery, celery, broccoli, broccoli, asparagus,
   asparagus and squash! and squash!
He was mad, he was mad,
He was bad, he was bad,
That bull, that bull,
In Trinidad, in Trinidad.
Tch tch tch tch tch.....

93

THESE BONES SHALL RISE AGAIN

1. The Lord, he thought he'd make a man
   These bones shall rise again
   He took a little water and a little sand
   These bones shall rise again
   I know it brother, I know it brother,
      I know it, brother
   These bones shall rise again

2. He thought he's make a woman too
   These bones shall rise again
   He did not know just what to do
   These bones shall rise again
   I know it, brother, I know it, brother,
      I know it, brother
   These bones shall rise again

3. He took a rib from Adam's side
   These bones shall rise again
   He said this bone shall be your bride
   These bones shall rise again
   I know it, brother, I know it, brother,
      I know it, brother
   These bones shall rise again

4. Now that Adam has a wife
   These bones shall rise again
   He'll be happy all of his life
   These bones shall rise again
   I know it, brother, I know it,
      brother, I know it, brother
   These bones shall rise again

5. This is where my story ends
   No-o-o-
   But we'll always be good friends
   Ah-ah-ah-
   I know it, brother, I know it,
      brother, I know it, brother
   We'll sing our songs again
   We'll sing our songs again
   We'll sing our songs again

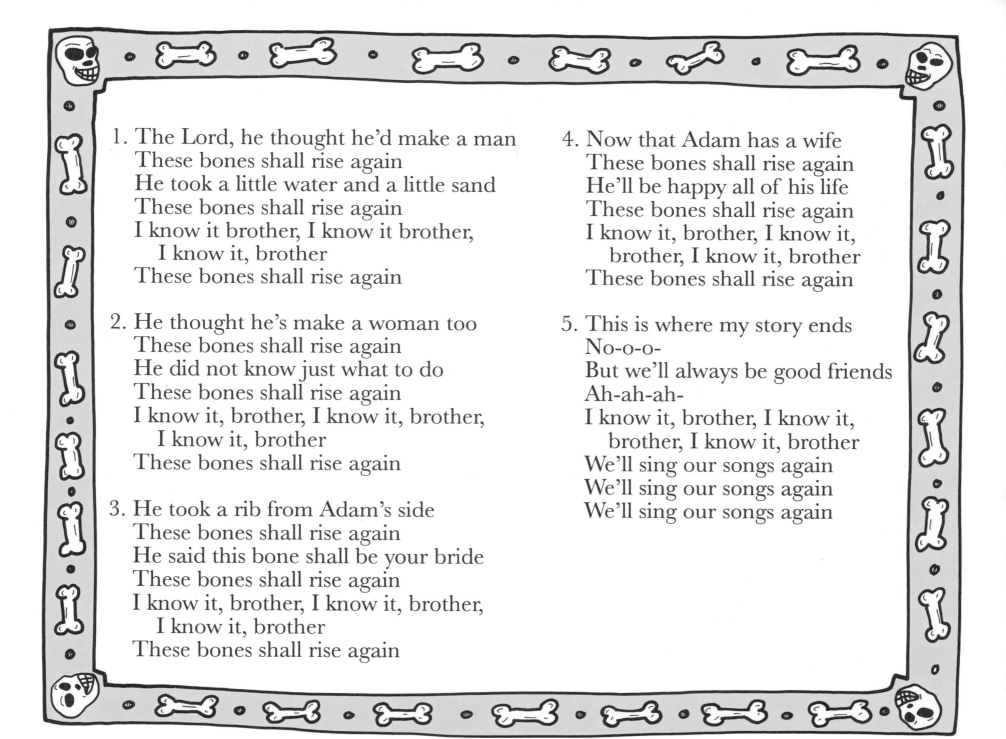

Langston Hughes, an African American poet, speaks of **rhythm**:

"**Rhythm** is something we share in common, **you** and **I**, with all the **plants** and **animals** and **people** in the world, and with the **stars** and **moon** and **sun**, and all the whole vast **wonderful universe** beyond this wonderful **earth** which is our **home**."

This is the **end** and this is the **beginning** and **THIS IS RHYTHM**